SHINE AND SHADOW

SHINE AND SHADOW

Meditations

KATHLEEN MCTIGUE

SKINNER HOUSE BOOKS

BOSTON

Printed in the United States

Cover and text design by Suzanne Morgan
Author photo by Bruce Levison

print ISBN: 978-1-55896-621-5
eBook ISBN: 978-1-55896-622-2

6 5 4 3 2 1
13 12 11

"Ten Thousand Baby Names" is adapted from a version printed in the *New Haven Register* on April 28, 2008.

"The Parents' Pilgrimage" is adapted from a version printed in *UU World* in July/August 1999 and also *The Family Therapy Networker* on July 1, 1999.

Library of Congress Cataloging-in-Publication Data

McTigue, Kathleen.
  Shine and shadow : meditations / Kathleen McTigue.
      p. cm.
ISBN 978-1-55896-621-5 (pbk. : alk. paper)—ISBN 978-1-55896-622-2 (ebook) 1. Meditations. 2. Spiritual life—Unitarian Universalist Association. 3. Devotional calendars. I. Title.
  BX9855.M44 2011
  242—dc23
                              2011017686

For Nick, Sam, Hannah, and Maris—
my sustenance and inspiration;
and for the members of the
Unitarian Society of New Haven—
my companions and teachers.

CONTENTS

NEW YEAR'S DAY

It's five below zero, too cold to go out
yet you do go, into the envelope of light
that holds this winter morning.

Iced air needles your soft mouth,
    aches on your teeth;
trees engrave themselves black against
    the brilliant sky,
then again, blue relief scratched
on the sheets of snow
and the thin crust of ice sends a sheen and shattering
of sun back into the curve of cloudless sky.

On the shoveled walk the snow creaks
beneath your boots
then you're out in the deep froth of it
hoisting the seed bucket and your awkward body
    through the stillness,
wishing you were lighter
to pass like the blue shadows
and leave no sign.

When you finish and turn
a chickadee lights, puffed fat against the cold,
his black eyes shining a query of hunger, waiting.

Soon you'll go back into the easy warmth
where the sun pours gold through the windows
and the two lazy cats follow it all day

from couch to carpet to ottoman;
you will sit with them, steam rising from your tea
as you watch the birds quarrel and fuss.

But now you stand still in this shine and shadow,
and note the small drum of your heartbeat, the swirl
of ice against your tongue as you breathe.

January—The years turn
    one into the next so swiftly, your age
has come sifting down on you unnoticed, and surely
there are more bright beads
    already threaded for you than await
in that glimmering pile the world spills out as it
spools around the sun—

but the light of this day, the frozen air,
the black eye of a small bird, waiting—
what peace, though time is passing,
drifts lightly like a friend's arm settling
around your shoulders.

HOW TO GIVE A BLESSING

We're asked a dozen times a day, "How are you?" Most of the time it's not a real question and doesn't invite a genuine answer. It's more like an alternative "hello," and we're well-trained in the ritual response: "Fine, thanks."

But every once in a while we are asked this question when things are really not fine at all. At those times—when we're walking around in a little bubble of anxiety or sorrow—something inside us can suddenly balk at giving out the standard, meaningless answer. We are too hungry for an authentic word, too raw to pretend that things are okay.

The morning after my father died, following three days and nights of an around-the-clock vigil with my siblings, I had to go to the grocery store to buy a few things for dinner. When I arrived at the check-out counter and the clerk distractedly said, "How are you?" my brain went blank. I couldn't say "fine," or even "okay." I wasn't okay. I wasn't even in my right mind. I was numb, sleep-deprived, and saturated with the mystery of our mortality. That's the only explanation I have, because to my horror I found myself blurting out a real and honest answer. "I'm not so good," I said. "My Dad died last night."

With his hands filled with the apples, chicken, and bread, the poor clerk turned red and started to stammer. The people behind me looked longingly at the check-out lines they should have chosen, the ones that would not have placed them in earshot of the too-much-information lady. I was mortified at having revealed to an unprepared stranger just how not-fine I was. Everyone froze in this moment of uncomfortable paralysis—except the young man bagging the groceries, who had Down's syndrome. He stopped moving completely, looked straight at me, and with a little slur and great emphasis said, "I bet you feel really sad about that."

The simplicity of that little expression of kindness and solidarity allowed both the clerk and me to escape. "Yes, I do. Thank you," I said to him, and then I was able to walk out with my groceries and not feel quite so much as though I had just undressed in public. I thought about that encounter for a long time. The young man bagging groceries would be considered disabled, in thought, speech, and movement. Yet he was the only one able to offer what counted in that particular moment: He knew how to give a blessing.

WINTER BLESSING

The world catches our hearts through its light:
    splintering dance of sun on water,
    calm moonlight poured through branches,
    candles lit on early winter evenings,
    a spatter of stars on a clear night,
    and the bright eyes of those we love.
But the brilliance never ends,
    even when the light goes out.
Mystery shimmers and shines in the world
    in even the darkest corners.
It's there where the roots push life into soil and rock,
    in small lives lived under every stone;
    there in the silent pulse beneath the tree bark.
It's in the depth of slow tides as they turn,
    there in the sky on moonless nights
    when muffling clouds block out the stars.
It's there in the prison, the hospital,
    by the hospice bed,
    there at the graveside, in the empty house—

something beating in the dark shelter
    of our hearts—
the small shine of hope, the gilt edge of kindness.

May we be granted the gift of deeper sight
that we might see—with or without the light.

To learn something by heart is not the same as memorization. Back in elementary school I memorized the multiplication tables up through twelve. I also committed to memory the correct spelling for words like *atrocious*, which I still retain, and the capitals for all fifty states, which I do not.

There were other things I learned not through memorizing, but by heart. One of these was how to bake bread, following the same unwritten recipe my mother had learned from her own mother. Working next to her in a fragrant kitchen, I absorbed this knowledge not only by listening to her instructions but through touch, scent, and taste. I learned by heart the look and smell of yeast as it came to life, the stretch and pull of a good solid dough under the heel of the hand, the enveloping welcome of a home scented with fresh-baked bread, and the rough kiss of a warm crust on the lips. What we learn by heart enters us so deeply that it is incorporated, embodied, not just remembered. It becomes a part of who we are.

My friend Shirley visits her elderly mother several times a week. For many years now her mother has drifted on the dark tides of Alzheimer's disease, so lost in that inner landscape that she passes weeks at a time without speaking a word. So it was quite a shock when Shirley walked in to visit one day and her mother looked at her sharply and declared that she needed to go shopping. Startled to hear her mother speak at all, Shirley responded with the first thing that popped into her head: "Mother, what do you need to get?" The answer came back, "A pie plate."

Intrigued and bemused, Shirley took her hand and tried to enter the place where her mother's mind had momentarily come back to life. "You want to make a pie? What kind?" Her mother murmured, "apple pie," and then closed her eyes and seemed to drift away again into her illness. A moment later she looked up into her daughter's face. Speaking each word with careful deliberation, she said, "Apples. Flour. Crisco. Salt. Sugar. Cinnamon." Shirley's mother learned how to bake pies as a very little girl, standing at her own mother's side, and she never used a recipe. She had learned it all by heart.

If we live long enough, the time will come to each of us when the bright fires of our minds begin to dim and settle, perhaps until only a few coals still linger there at the end of our lives, still gleaming with a bit of light. That's where we'll hold the knowledge of the few things we've most loved doing in the gifted flow of life, the things we've learned not just through our minds but through taste, touch, and scent. The things we learned by heart.

TRUE WISDOM

In the famous illustration of King Solomon's wisdom, two women came to him fighting over an infant. Each had given birth to a baby boy just days before, and they were sleeping in the same room together when one of the babies died during the night. Awakening to this calamity, the mother of the dead baby switched the two and claimed the living one as her own, but the other mother knew her child and refused to give him up. They came to the king for resolution.

Solomon listened to the argument and then called for his sword. He told the women that since there was no way to know which of them was telling the truth, he would simply divide the baby equally—as though they were fighting over a loaf of bread!—and they could each take half. One of the women agreed, but the other immediately cried out, "No, no! Give her the baby, don't kill him!" Solomon of course gave the baby to that woman, the one who preferred to lose the fight and the baby rather than see him killed. The story ends with these words: "All Israel stood in awe of the king, because they perceived that the wisdom of God was in him."

I was a little kid the first time I heard this hair-raising story and, unlike all of Israel, I didn't stand in awe of the king but in terror of what might have happened. What if the real mother hadn't spoken soon enough, or had said the wrong thing? Would the king have gone through with it, just to make his point? I imagined the tiny baby with a cold sword poised over him, and it all seemed terribly unfair and cruel. And what about the mother of the baby who died in the night? I kept wondering what happened to her after Solomon revealed her deceit and humiliated her so publicly.

Clearly, I had an overactive imagination as a child! But all my questions really added up to this: What good is a clever solution that comes without kindness? If this story is going to stand as an example of wisdom, we have to imagine it continuing on past the sword that frightens the truth from a couple of anguished mothers.

If he's going to be lifted up as a paragon of wisdom, we should expect a little more of Solomon. Let the rightful mother have her baby, gloriously alive and intact, but then let the king be wise in heart as well as head, so that when he looks at the other woman he sees more than just a liar caught in the act. Let him see a mother out of her mind with grief and loss. Let her presence remind Solomon of his own lies, his own unbearable losses, and so bring him off his throne and down on his knees next to her where she huddles. Let him speak some word of kindness, then lift her up and walk with her, back to the cold room where her deepest fear and sorrow lies wrapped in a still bundle on the bed. Let him stay with her there, quietly, to help bear this most grievous of losses, a dead child.

If it's wisdom we're after, we must remember that the truest wisdom comes laced through with compassion, as we come to know how alike we are—each of us doing our best to find the path ahead and to keep on walking with our fragile, broken hearts. And all of us in deep need of each other's kindness.

BATHING IN STARLIGHT

It was the end of a hectic day and the start of the kind of evening familiar to anyone who's juggling work and young children. Time is the enemy, relentlessly streaming past, leaving in its wake an endless clutter of unfinished tasks. Like a flustered hen in a barnyard, I clucked and fretted as I hustled my children along through homework, dinner, bath time and bedtime stories, always trying to get things to move a little faster against the ticking clock.

With the kids finally in bed a half-hour later than I'd aimed for, I fussed my way out the door to give the dog her walk, bustling along as my fretful mind danced through a dozen other still unfinished chores. I was halfway down the driveway before I glanced up. My jaw dropped—there before me the whole spread of the Milky Way splintered out across the clear black sky, stars behind stars in the deep pool of space. And then I finally stood still, washed in starlight that had been traveling toward me for millions of years. I was brought to my senses, and very nearly brought to my knees.

Because bedtime had been late, my children were still awake. To their delighted surprise, the mother hen reappeared in their bedroom doorways, no longer clucking, and carried them one at a time, pajamas and all, out into the crisp winter air to bathe in that ancient light.

Maybe this is all we can bear of the cosmic perspective on time, this little glimpse of eternity that lets us see our small lives connected to everything else on so massive a scale. My awe at the immensity revealed in a clear night sky doesn't leave me feeling diminished or irrelevant. Instead it reminds me that if we can be present exactly in the moment we are living, we can step outside of time altogether. We live immersed in that eternity, after all—we just forget, until something like starlight wakes us up to it again.

THE DUCK OF ENLIGHTENMENT

One spring afternoon I went home a little early so I could claim an hour of study time before my children got home. As I opened the door, I was greeted by both cats, which was a little odd because they don't usually condescend to notice our coming and going unless it's dinner time. One of them promptly bolted out the open door while the other wrapped himself persistently around my legs. As I stood puzzling over this behavior, at the edge of my vision I caught a sudden motion in the family room where there should be no motion at all in the empty house. With the hair rising on the back of my neck I slowly moved into the house and rounded the corner of the room, and then I saw it. There was a duck in the family room. A wild brown duck—a *live* duck. In the family room.

My brain actually stopped completely for a couple of heartbeats. What should the brain do, after all, with so utterly unexpected a sight? I stood there in the doorway and said out loud, *"There is a duck in the family room,"* as though it would help me believe it. None of the windows were open. The doors were properly closed. The duck huddled in the far corner of the room next to a clutter of books and DVDs, radiating the hope that if she kept perfectly still I wouldn't see her. Carefully I caught her up—a small wood duck, female, her heart tapping frantically against my hands—and carried her outside. I looked at her, full of wonder for this little visitation. Then I opened my hands. She leapt into the air in a great arc of liberation and beat her wings in a straight line of escape all the way to the horizon.

I went back inside to investigate the breach of household security, and within a few minutes the mystery was explained. A trail of ashes spilled from the fireplace, and here and there on the wall and against the ceiling I saw soot in little feather-shaped impressions where the duck had thrown herself up toward the light. It all made sense then, how a duck could come to be standing in the middle of my house. But I felt lucky that for the space of a few breaths, my linear, deductive mind had been shocked into silence. When something tumbles us into that state of wonder, the unexpected quiet in our heads is like a window flung open on the world. Instead of the routine, predictable story we live each day, there is something new under the sun and, sur- prised out of our minds for a moment, we actually *see*. Startled awake, we receive what's in front of us: simple, astonishing, unedited.

Afterward, basking in the dazzlement of my visi- tor, it occurred to me that it really shouldn't require a duck in the family room to awaken my wonder. Isn't the same lovely little wood duck just as won- drous, just as worthy of my awe and my open and grateful heart, when she is out in the woods where she belongs? The real miracle is not that her frightened heart beat against my hands for a moment but that her heart beats at all—that her heart beats, that my hands can hold, that my eyes can see.

I have an article from an old Irish newspaper, the *Belfast Newsletter*. Written in 1849, the story tells about the loss of a ship full of immigrants, just as it approached the coast of Canada at the end of its long voyage from Ireland. In the breathless, dramatic prose of his era, the reporter writes, "Late at night the ship ran into an iceberg with terrific force. The whole of her bows were stove in, and the next moment the sea was rushing into the hold with the violence of a cataract. . . . About twenty of the passengers managed to reach the deck just before she went down, some of whom jumped onto the ice while others clung to the floating spars. Nine only, however, could be preserved—six men, two women, and a boy. One hundred and nine unhappy souls perished."

The account ends with the names of those unlikely nine who managed to survive, and among them is the little boy, Patrick McTigue, my grandfather's grandfather. A second cousin unearthed the article in Ireland and sent it around to family members. We had always heard the tale that there was a shipwreck in our past, but by the time it had reached even my father's generation it was told with a dubious tone and no details. Maybe it happened and maybe it didn't; after all, every family likes to think of itself as special, escaping a gruesome fate by the skin of its collective teeth.

The thing is, it's always true, for every person, for every family. If we trace the delicate filament of life back far enough, we will each find the shipwreck, earthquake, landslide, pogrom, war, or starvation an ancestor barely escaped. And there will be close calls and near misses as well: the wartime bullet that spared your grandfather's heart by an inch; the chance meeting on an accidental road that led to your parents' marriage; the lucky moment when their love resulted in the particular pregnancy that led to the specific *you*. Hundreds of threads of connection bring us into life, each one unimaginably tenuous and fragile.

Nothing about our lives is ordinary. Held up against the shadows of pathways not taken, countless catastrophes could have snuffed out the spark that led to this beating heart, these wondrous hands. Every life is gift and grace; fragile, astonishing, and unrepeatable. We forget this easily, swept up in the pulse and busyness of our days. We hustle along with our private preoccupations, brows furrowed in concentration, hurrying lest we waste even a minute. But all of the important "doings" that fill our days pale against our singular "being." If we could remember this once in a while—if we could stop and simply marvel at the stupendous luck that has allowed each of us to live—perhaps we would live more gently with one another, more kindly and compassionately, as one survivor to another.

PASSOVER

When the escape from Egypt was certain, when the
last furious wave had closed over their enemies'
heads and the dangerous waters lay smooth again,
when the Israelites could finally turn toward the
future without fear that the past would snatch them
back—what did they see before them? Not the
Promised Land, flowing with milk and honey, but
the wide and terrifying wilderness that would claim
them for forty long, hard years of wandering. They
were not carried along on a surge of vindicated
faith, but stumbled forward with paralyzing doubts.
And instead of enjoying sweet unity after all they'd
been through, they were torn by bickering and divi-
sion. They walked into relentless uncertainty and
discomfort, and fell asleep on the hard ground to
wake feeling ashamed for dreaming of the easier life
of slavery they had left behind.

Our own stories will never be quite so dramatic.
Yet each of us knows a little about what it means to
be lost in the wilderness. We know the awful dis-
appointment, akin to despair, of being suddenly
pathless and alone when we'd expected to stride
confidently straight into the promised land. We
know how it feels to take a leap of faith toward some
place we want to be—in love or relationship, in work
or school or location—only to find that nothing

turns out the way we'd hoped and expected. The familiar has been left behind, but what we yearn for has not yet come into view, and there we are, lost in the desert. We have no way to know how long our wandering will last.

These passages through the land of in-between are scary and uncomfortable, and the desert is a place we would rather barrel through as quickly as possible toward the welcoming ground of our destination. But our time in the desert is a passage of the heart, not a physical journey of the body, and it's not in our power to speed it up.

I have never been lost in a literal desert, but there was a time in my life when I visited one every year. When I lived in the San Francisco area, every spring for five years I traveled with a friend to the low desert just over the California border into Arizona, where we camped for a week in the middle of nowhere. Every year the experience was the same: At first, especially after the damp lushness of the Bay Area, the landscape seemed absolutely barren and dead. Then my eyes would adjust, and I'd start to notice all the complicated forms of life that thrived there. The dryness of the air made things crystal clear even at great distances, and the desert light drew breathtaking colors out of the rocks and shadows. At night, there were the incredible desert stars.

I hold my lessons from the Southwestern desert close to my heart. They can sustain me through the deserts of the heart and soul when I wander the wilderness of in-between. Our inner deserts have something to offer us, too. It's hard to fight the impulse to get out of the place of passage as quickly as possible, but each day we spend there, no matter how uncomfortable, is a precious day of our lives. What strange gifts might it offer to us, if we can calm ourselves enough to look?

After forty years in the desert, the Israelites in the ancient myth finally reached its end. They touched life-giving waters again, and waded into the Jordan, amazed and glad. Maybe they knew, even in that moment of deep relief and readiness, that the desert wasn't accidental, that it had opened and cleansed them in some necessary way. Maybe they understood how the wilderness had sharpened their awareness and softened their hearts, so they could at long last receive, not just the gifts of the promised land, but the gifts of the desert that had brought them there.

The Easter story as told in the Gospel of John revolves around the experience of one person, Mary Magdalene. It's Mary who gets up before dawn on the day after the Jewish Sabbath and goes alone to visit the tomb. Her beloved teacher has died a horrible death, and it was only by the unexpected generosity of a wealthy man that Jesus was given even the small, late dignity of a real burial place instead of a pauper's grave. Because of the Sabbath, his body had not been cleaned according to tradition, and Mary set out early with her herbs in order to do this last grieving service. But when she got to the tomb she found that the stone blocking its entrance had already been rolled away, and his body was gone.

It isn't hard to imagine her despair and anger at being robbed of even this last farewell. She ran to some of Jesus' other followers with the news, and they came back with her to see for themselves. They probably stood there for a while arguing about what to do, but there was nothing to be done. Who would you complain to when you risked your life even admitting to the authorities that you had known him? Filled with that bitter realization, they finally left again.

But Mary stayed, alone and weeping; maybe something defiant crept in with her grief that made her brave enough to stay. Then she caught a movement out of the corner of her eye, and turned to find someone standing there. "Why are you crying?" he asked. "Who are you looking for?" Thinking he must be the gardener, she said, as carefully as she could, "Sir, if you have carried him away, tell me where you've put him and I'll take care of it. I won't tell anyone. I'll just take his body and clean him up so he can rest in peace." Then Jesus—because of course it was Jesus standing there, and she didn't recognize him—Jesus just called out her name: "Mary." And then she knew, and she said back to him, "Rabbi."

For those of us who believe that Jesus was a human being like us, the idea of his literal resurrection from death is a leap of faith we can't quite make. We know that when our bodies die, they die. We belong to the earth, and it is comforting and right to know that we dissolve again into that sweetness. But we can believe in Mary's resurrection. When Mary heard her name called, suddenly her eyes were opened to a new reality. She was called out from the blindness of her grief and despair, and from within herself she found a new way to see and to understand what had happened to her.

I take that Easter story as truth. It points to the moments in every life when something within us is called out, called forth, called to a deeper understanding of our world. Easter raises the question:

In this bright opening of the earth, in this turning season when new life is pouring out all around us, what will we bring forth from within ourselves? It's a time that calls us to open our eyes in a new way, to see not just what we expect to see but perhaps some bright and mysterious truth we could not fathom before, something completely new and unexpected.

We are a troubled tribe, we human beings. The unfolding story of our time on earth is clouded with pain and cruelty, with missed opportunities, unthinkable heedlessness, and indifference. It is also marked by the bright notes of decency, kindness, freedom, and courage. Easter proclaims that we each have a part to play in how the story unfolds, if we are willing to wake up. We listen for what is calling to us, and like Mary, when we hear our name we answer, rising anew to meet the life that will not stop calling our names.

THINKING LIKE A STONE

My Aunt Mary has lived alone much of her life in a little prospector's cabin far inside the boundaries of Yellowstone Park as a park biologist. She's a bit eccentric, and also remarkably wise to the ways of the earth. For as long as I can remember, she has said that she thinks like a stone. She doesn't mean that she sits around listening to rocks as they wax eloquent in subtle, gravelly voices. She means that she has learned to anchor herself in geologic time. She observes the seasons keenly as they come and go, but she is tuned into rhythms that are unfathomably long—sweeps of time that the stones know, counted not by years or even centuries, but by eons.

This gives my Aunt Mary an unshakable equanimity, right alongside her passion for the environment. She works tirelessly against the earth's degradation, but she thinks like a stone—and in geologic time, trees are a recent invention, the dinosaurs came and went just last week, and the whole span of human life has happened in the blink of a stony eye. With her consciousness anchored in this long and rocky view, my aunt says that the planet will survive us, no matter what we do—and will live well past our extinction. That's what gives rise to her serenity.

I find it very hard to think like a stone. I think like a human being, like a mother who wants to believe that her great-grandchildren will have a green earth to walk on, sweet air to breathe, the chance to see an osprey fishing in a lake, and to hear peepers trill out their awakening in the spring. However, this is where my aunt's wisdom might nevertheless wear off on me. If we can learn to think like a stone, then we might learn to think as though we are truly a part of the planet instead of merely living on it. We might learn to see with a sort of double vision that allows us our love and loyalty to our own kin but stretches us beyond them as well. With that dual vision, we can start to live as though it is not human life that should be the measure of all things—it is the planet's life. We might learn not only to think like a stone, but to also think like an American chestnut or an elm, to think like a peeper, a cicada, a hawk or a red fox, a vulture, a coral reef, or an Amazon butterfly. We might come to believe that their lives on earth actually matter as much as our own.

Thinking like a stone, we begin to know the truth at a bone-deep level that we are not living *on* the earth, we *are* the earth, as everything else is the earth, rising into life in wild, extravagant variety and all made of the same handful of minerals, chemicals, and salty water into which we will dissolve when we die. We are the earth made conscious, a unique and marvelous way in which the earth itself can see, reflect, contemplate, and choose. The stones of our planet have been around for a long, long time, and they will be here as long as our bright little jewel of an earth keeps spinning around the sun. If we want life to continue blossoming among those stones, we've got to take on their long view—and then use our marvelous large brains to benefit the bright planet that gave rise to them in the first place.

TEN THOUSAND BABY NAMES

When my youngest daughter was about two years old she came across a tattered paperback on our bookshelves, *Ten Thousand Baby Names*, and for a little while this was her favorite book. Drawn by the shining face of the baby on the cover, she brought it to me over and over and demanded that I read through the names. This was prelude to what was, at the time, her favorite story of all: How we chose her name.

What's in a name? Always, there is a story. You were named for a beloved relative or, contrarily, named after no one because your parents wanted a clean break from family history. If you were a first son and your family went in for such things, you got to be called after your father and have "junior" tacked on. If you were a daughter, you could be named for a virtue or aspiration such as Hope, Serenity, or Faith. Recalling some sweet romantic setting, your parents might have named you for their favorite Spanish or Italian village. Perhaps you carry the name of one of their heroes or heroines, or more whimsically, some favorite musician or movie star. Maybe you've ended up with an affectionate nickname born of a sibling's mispronunciation, or some jackass thing you tried as an adolescent and never lived down.

Always, there is a story.

In church on Sunday mornings we read aloud the names of the American soldiers killed in Iraq or Afghanistan each week. Alone in my study the night before, I speak each name out loud and then wonder about the stories. I imagine these soldiers as the babies they once were, held in someone's arms at a baptism or naming ceremony. The proud relatives gathered around as the name was formally bestowed, and everyone beamed as the baby cooed or wailed or fidgeted. There was so much gladness and pride in each moment of naming, and not once did anyone imagine that the road their baby walked would end eighteen or twenty years later in a mix of blood and dust halfway around the world.

As part of a witness for peace on Memorial Day, a cairn of stones was built at a busy downtown intersection in Hartford, each stone bearing the name of a fallen American soldier, or one of the tens of thousands of Iraqi and Afghani civilians who have died in these wars. How do you choose one name from thousands, to symbolize so much carnage and loss? I finally brought three stones to the cairn, one for each of my own three children. Each stone bore the name of a child who had died on the birthday of one of mine. As I placed the stones, I wondered about their names. Always, there is a story.

HOLY AMBIVALENT

The year I turned thirty was a tricky one for me. I was unsettled in all the largest areas of my life: vocation, location, and relationship. Decisions loomed, each one feeling huge, portentous, and muddled up with the other choices facing me. In the midst of this decision-making turmoil and angst, I took a trip to southern Mexico, where I spent some time in the little town of San Cristobal. I was drawn to the town's old churches, where I felt comfort and a sense of holiness simply because they held within their walls centuries of human longing and hope.

One morning I walked into my favorite of these churches and sat in the front pew breathing the musty peace of the place. The ornate altar was full of candles, each one lit by someone's hope or yearning. Then a dozen people entered, local men and women who wore the beautiful, bright woven clothes of that area. They were led by an older man dressed in white, and they all came to the altar and knelt on the stone floor in front of me. I watched as the leader made supplications and prayed for fifteen minutes, not in the Spanish I knew but an indigenous tongue I couldn't fathom.

After a short, expectant silence he then turned and took the wrist of the woman sitting next to him. He bowed his head for a moment; then looked into her face and began to speak quietly, only to her. One by one he did the same thing for each person in the group: took a wrist, bowed tenderly over it in silence, and then spoke with quiet certainty, each person listening intently, nodding.

It dawned on me that this man was a diviner, and that he held each person's wrist with his thumb on the pulse point. After listening to the secrets of their hearts, he looked into each face with authority and wisdom, and spoke the truth he discerned. As I watched this ceremony and the kind face of this man from out of my private fog of doubt and indecision, I found myself filled with yearning. I wanted nothing in the world more than to have him cradle my wrist in his hand, and bow his head to listen with his inner ear for the direction my life ought to take. Then he would turn those eyes on me and speaking in a language I could understand, say, "This is what you should do." I would listen and nod, everything suddenly clear, and then I'd be on my way, free of doubt.

But it didn't happen. The holy man never caught my eye, and I didn't try to cross the barriers of language, culture, and belief to ask him to listen to my beating heart. Instead I walked back out into the flat, hot sunlight and the practical streets of San Cristobal, full of ordinary people dealing with life's unknowns and making their choices. Eventually, through the course of time and struggle, I made the decisions that faced me then and went on to the next ones, and the next.

We all come to some decision points when every option seems ambiguous, and we don't have a clue which way to go. We arrive at a turn in the road that we can't see around until we take the next steps forward, and we take those steps not knowing whether we've made the right choice. We continue on a wing and a prayer, but sometimes, if we can be still, if we can stop our anxious dithering and wait quietly, we'll hear our heart's wisdom. It's beating there at the pulse-point, waiting for us to listen.

SNAPSHOTS

My friend Art is in frail health now, well into his
eighties, but in his younger years he was a vigorous
hiker. One day he made the trek up Mount Adams
alone. As he sat at the summit drinking in the view
and munching a sandwich, he turned to find an
elderly woman slowly huffing and puffing her way
up the last of the trail. They greeted each other and
she plopped down with a great sigh of relief. After
she'd caught her breath, she didn't comment on the
spectacular view; she didn't even look at it. Instead,
she pulled out her camera and began snapping photos at a furious pace, turning as she did in order to
capture the whole horizon.

Dumbfounded, Art watched her for a little while
and then had to ask. "Uh . . . Do you always take
photos like this?" The woman cheerfully replied,
"Oh, always! You see, I still love to hike and to get
up to the best views, but I'm going blind, and since I
can't really see it anymore I take a ton of photos.
I have them developed when I get back down. Then I
hold them up really close to my eyes, and that way
I can see where I've been!"

Memory is a little like this. Like the woman using
her snapshots to see where she's been, we lift up to
our mind's eye a sampling of moments from the
millions through which we've lived. The sweetest

memories are the ones we hold up most often, but sometimes a random memory of some long-ago and ordinary day becomes treasured with the passage of time, symbolic of a whole sweep of years long past.

We remember those we've loved this way too— as a composite, because a person is too vast and complex to hold in the memory in totality. Instead, we hold them as snapshots. You remember a particular angle of the head, a unique crinkle in the lines around the eyes, the wicked contagiousness of his laugh, the tenderness in her voice when she spoke your name. You remember the specific fleck of light in the brown of his eyes, the lovely smell right at the base of her neck, the way he held the baby, the movement of her hands as she shaped the pie crust.

This is what is left behind. They are just snapshots, so small when held up to the richness of a life, and yet they fill us. The essence of who we loved is captured there, in these fragments. They show us a little bit of where we have been, but more important they show us *who* we have been, and lead us on toward who we're still becoming.

SUMMER SABBATH

Go someplace you haven't seen before,
where no one knows you, where you don't think twice
about what to wear, how you look, or who might be
    watching
as you let your body ease out into the sun and bask,
    lazy as a cat.

Untether yourself from the engines of busyness, one
    by one—
laptop, desktop, wristwatch, scribbled lists,
even the telephone,
especially the one you carry everywhere,
the little tyrant.
This will all feel unnatural
but it's not.

Sit by water—
a place where the sea comes in
warm as a breath,
where the crest of each nighttime wave catches the
    moon
and spreads it out again, lavish, on the sand;

or a little stream in the mountains
where a hundred tumbling voices burble and blend
in your quieting mind until behind them
you almost hear a choir of wood angels, humming;

or a still lake outside your grandfather's cabin,
water lapping so lightly
you can barely make out its tongue rasping the sand,
shores ringed by pine and sweet cedar
and beyond them high mountains in their silence.

Go and don't think about time:
how much you've got left,
how to pass, fill, use or spend it,
whether you might accidentally lose or waste it,
and certainly never entertain the thought that time
is money. It's not.

Instead, consider your life—
who you love, and why,
how blessed you are to be here, resting
under a shower of birdsong,
or what strange bright luck it is to be the owner,
for a few years, of this beating heart,
these wondering eyes, the ears
into which the kingfisher spills her small chuckle
as she dips across the water.

You might ponder these things, but you could also let
the whole creaking apparatus of thought come to a
    halt.
You might surrender, and let the world spill in
    through the five gates,

no sentry standing surly watch,
no one left to resist or defend.

The innermost courtyard stands empty then,
a clear fountain singing at the center.

EXTREME MAKEOVER

Why is there such a difference between the way we look at a baby's body and the way we look at our own? When it comes to babies, we feel pure delight in everything we see: the little shell of an ear, the sweet cheeks and bump of a nose, each tiny fingernail, the smooth, pudgy bottom, the delicious thighs with their folds of baby fat.

Most of us don't turn even a fraction of that admiration and joy toward our own bodies. Instead, we look at them with dissatisfaction, even distaste. We find our bodies too fat or short, too gangly or round, our breasts too big or small. We study our faces critically. We see our noses as flawed—hooked or crooked, too bulbous, or too pointy. Our ears stick out. Our eyes are too close together. We've learned to see the body as something to be plucked, shaved, and manicured, wrestled with to make it slimmer, worked out to make its muscles bulge or its bottom tight. We disguise, paint, and dye it to make it look thinner, younger, and more luminous. As we get older, even the truly gorgeous among us start to measure ourselves by what we are not. We fret that we are no longer young and our sags and folds distress us.

Once while waiting my turn in a doctor's office, a magazine caught my eye with a cover article promising details on "Extreme Make-Overs." Maybe my mind had been drifting or maybe my aversion to TV has left me thoroughly out of the mainstream, but I swear to you that when I picked it up, I thought the article would be about people who had radically changed their life situation by some heroic internal transformation. I imagined someone moving from a lengthy prison term for drunk driving into becoming a counselor for substance abusers.

Of course, the article instead recounted a whole package of surgeries women had undergone—their lips pooched out and puffy eyes made sleek, bellies tucked and shrunk, breasts made perky, thighs made slim. All with raving commentary from the women themselves about how fine and dandy their lives will be, now that they don't look so old, fat, or saggy.

This kind of surgery as a bizarre spectator sport may be the inevitable outcome of our culture's attitude toward beauty and aging, but I wonder about the women who put themselves there under the knife. Surely before too long, their unhappiness will surface again in some other guise. There is no surgery, no matter how radical or expensive, that will keep us from getting old, from eventually becoming sick or disabled, or from dying when our time comes. There is no surgery that teaches us to listen to the body's hungers and needs, to treasure our cunning fingers and our humble feet as they touch the world, to take joy in how we move to pulsing rhythms when we dance or to appreciate how sturdily our thighs carry us up the mountain path.

So the extreme makeover we really need is one that happens to our minds, not our bodies. A change that lets us love and honor our flesh as it is, even as our bodies are worn down and used up by the lives we lead. A makeover so extreme that we might even bow to the body's failings as they come, and keep ourselves grateful, without regret, for what is still ours—all the ways the world touches us, enters us, through the gateways of the body.

BREATHING PEACE INTO BEING

This is a house of peace.
Breathe in a grateful breath that you sit here
this moment of your life
    safely, and in silence.

There is a war raging,
    far from this place of comfort.
We know it is there, we know our brothers and sisters
    suffer its poisonous touch.
Our hearts are weighted with what we cannot resolve—
    with the knowledge that we do not have a way
    to call a halt,
    to step into the fury with the flag
    of no nation but peace, the one banner
    that calls equally in every language.

So here we lift its promise in our own souls,
and remember that in this place, in this moment,
    we are not at war.
Breathe in the truth of this moment:
here is our strength, our deep well of courage.
Breathing in, we rest our spirits.
Breathing out, we pray for peace.

May those in harm's way be safe
    for another day.
May those who drive the engines of power
    be awakened by compassion.

May we all hold the cup filled with courage and will
that has been carried by peacemakers in long ages
before us.
May we drink of it deeply, and be steadfast
in the ways of peace.

BACKSIDE REDEMPTION

Each August my family vacations for two weeks in a cabin on Mount Desert Island in Maine. We often explore the back roads on bikes, and one early morning I set out on my own. I wanted to explore a new route I hoped would take me in a nice long loop, but I got lost. Just as I was steeling myself to turn around and retrace the long, uphill road back to the cabin, I pedaled around one last curve and saw two things simultaneously. First, a tiny white church, with a small, perfect steeple and bright red doors, and then the prominent sign with lovely, church-like calligraphy: "Backside Redemption."

I stopped, wheeled my bike to the side of the road, leaned on the handlebars and stared in awe at the sheer boldness of the declaration. Who were these people who could actually admit that the redemption they offered was the back-sided kind? A sort of come-as-you-are, seat-of-the-pants, possibly not-even-fit-for-good-society kind of redemption?

Then I saw the little recycling hut off to the side behind the church. Belatedly, I realized that the marvelous sign did not refer to the church at all but to the recycling hut, identified as "back side" because this part of the island faces the mainland, not the ocean. Sheepishly I looked around and spotted a smaller sign offering up the real name for the church, but by then it was too late. The little white building with its neatly painted red doors had forever sunk into my psyche as the "Backside Redemption Church."

This image has become a touchstone for me, a reminder that the only kind of redemption we ever really get is the backside kind, the kind that doesn't come in the package or on the schedule we have in mind. Like getting lost on my bike and then stumbling upon the church, it's backside redemption when a wrong turn takes us to a place that brings us up short and makes us stop and stare in amazement. Backside redemption can be waiting for us in the more drastic detours of our lives—such as the plans that don't materialize, the mistakes we make, the delays, disappointments and losses that somehow, over the long run, lead us to new insight and show us where we're really trying to go.

The little church and the recycling center offer a lovely serendipity—both have to do with redemption. What happens when we recycle bottles and cans? They are transformed; they are made into something else. Though it may seem a homely analogy for something as lofty as our souls, that's exactly what we're after. In our inconsistent and often clumsy ways, we're aiming for transformation.

Each time we take ourselves in hand and change our direction, ask forgiveness and start anew, we reaffirm our belief that we are redeemable. We don't want to stay exactly as we are. We don't want to keep being driven by the hair-trigger temper or the relentless, bitter grudge, or by our impatience or harsh judgments. We want to loosen the pinching in our hearts and live with more wonder, serenity, kindness, and wisdom. We want to live so there's a little shimmer of grace left behind when we're gone.

Backside redemption isn't straightforward or easy. It doesn't fall down on us from on high or come in a flash of illumination. It is filled with false starts and wrong turns, lessons we learn but then have to learn all over again. Backside redemption isn't about saving us, but instead *shaping* us, and it's the most certain redemption available in this sweet world.

THE ZEN OF PARENTING

Some years ago I went off for a brief meditation
retreat at the Buddhist center in Barre, Massachusetts.
Because of the twin demands of work and family
life, it took a lot of planning to get away even for a
few nights, so I was ready to treasure this chance for
a little silence and contemplation. But on the drive
up I felt anxious and jumpy. When I settled in at the
retreat center and sat down to meditate, ready to
drift away on a cloud of tranquility, my mind flooded
with disaster scenarios about my children. One after
another, I considered notions such as the babysitter
failing to be at the bus stop on time and a murderer
kidnapping one of my daughters, or a fire in the
middle of the night and no one waking up in time.
My husband might let go of a hand in a crowd and
my child would be lost forever. A car could careen
out of control or a catastrophic illness might strike.

This is not usually how I spend my quiet
moments, and it was shocking to have to pull myself
back from imagined catastrophe again and again.
Finally my mind settled down and the serenity of the
setting began to work on me. I looked with a little
more ease on the vast world of possibility that is out
of everyone's control, and knew that I wasn't alone
in my anxiety. At times each of us feels our fragile
hearts beat in fear for all that might befall those we

love so deeply. The world's gifts and its madness are both out of our hands, and we have no choice but to let go.

As I relaxed a little into that unchanging truth, I felt another sort of relinquishment. My children were growing up, sprouting long limbs and developing astounding vocabularies right before my eyes. Already I had lost them; they were not who they used to be. They were no longer the babies I nursed and cradled, the toddlers with their big bellies and earnest swaggers, the little boy who sucked his finger as he listened to the bedtime stories. How many years had it been since Sam wanted a bedtime story? When did Hannah stop asking for "Rockabye Baby" at night? When did Maris lose that persistent lisp when she tried to say the letter "R"?

Our children leave us again and again as they grow into new versions of themselves, shaking off the old self the way a snake sheds its skin. They don't want us to hold them to what they once liked or wanted. They don't want us to hold them to the behavior that was once so predictable. They don't want us to hold them back, and the day comes when they don't want us to hold them at all.

One recent evening as we lingered at the dinner table, our son Sam—now six feet tall—recounted something he used to do when he was seven or eight years old. Finished with his reminiscence he declared ruefully, "Boy, I was a weird little kid." I started to argue, leaping to the defense of that child he had been, not weird at all but a little boy, *my* boy. Then I realized how strange it was, defending his past self to this tall, confident young man that the little boy had become. He doesn't need me to defend him, or help him know himself. He's got that covered. He just needs me to love him still, in his present incarnation, and then to let that son go as well, in order to greet the one who will wake in our home tomorrow. Relinquishment is a difficult practice, but it's at the core of the spiritual path of parenting.

SABBATH HOME

Here in the refuge of this Sabbath home
we turn our busy minds toward silence,
and our full hearts toward one another.
We move together through the mysteries:
the bright surprise of birth and the shadowed
    questions of death.
In our slow walk between the two we will be wounded,
and we will be showered with grace,
    amazing, unending.
Even in our sorrows, we feel our lives
cradled in holiness we cannot comprehend,
and though we each walk within a vast loneliness,
the promise we offer here is that we do not walk alone.
This is a holy place in which we gather—
the light of the earth brought in and held,
    touched then
by our answering light:
the flame on a chalice,
the flicker of a candle,
the lamps of our open faces brought near.
In this place of silence and celebration,
solemnity and music,
we make a sanctuary and name our home.
Into this home we bring our hunger for awakening.
We bring compassionate hearts,
and a will toward justice.

Into this home we bring the courage to walk on
after hard losses.
Into this home we bring our joy,
and gratitude for ordinary blessings.
By our gathering we bless this place.
In its shelter we know ourselves blessed.

MENDING THE BROKEN WORLD

In early September I stop to watch my neighbor
at work repairing a stone wall that lines the road
perpendicular to ours. Built as all the old field walls
of our region have been built, the stones are held by
balance and judicious choice rather than by mortar.
The wall was built well, but the weight of many
decades has broken it here and there, with some
stones fallen out of place or carried away for some
other use.

As I warm myself in the autumn sun and watch
him work, I see that about half of what he does is
simply look at the stones in their haphazard piles,
stroking his chin in thought. Then from time to
time he rolls one from the pile onto the ground
and turns it from side to side, pondering, or walks
back to study again the place in the wall he's trying
to mend. When he finally makes his choice, he's sure.
Each stone waits for the right opening, the place
where its particular heft and shape fit as though
cradled. Once in place it is no longer merely a stone,
but an essential piece of the wall, part of a larger
thing taking shape as naturally as a tree flows from
root to trunk to branch.

My neighbor is an ordinary working man. I know
his name, and sometimes we talk together about
life and horses and his willingness to help me haul

manure to my garden one of these days before the first hard frost. But on this sunny September afternoon as I watch his eyes and hands become familiar with each stone and then lift it to shape the wall, it's easy to imagine God at work in the immense universe, quietly humming, pulling our lives together into something strong and useful.

I don't mean we're mute or helpless, waiting passively for the great Stonemason to lift and move our lives or tell us where we belong. I mean only that there is a place for us, that our gifts—the shape of our minds and talents, the angles of our interest and concern—fit the needs of the world the way my neighbor's stones anchor themselves in the lengthening wall. I mean that the world's possibilities shift and change each time we put ourselves into building something large and strong and beautiful. Whether or not we find room in our theologies for the word *God*, the world itself calls us to imagine ourselves essential to this engaged holiness, bringing forth what is ours to give of creation and strength, toward mending the broken world.

ONE QUIET THING AT A TIME

Today the woods dripped closed and cold
after nine long days of October rain;
the ground seemed to exhale mushroom and mold,

the weary grasses stood bent and tossed;
beaten leaves cluttered brown and dirty
clumped on the dying moss.

A wind pushed against me, insistent, chill,
bearing news that winter comes early now
sliding in over sere dark hills.

Perpetual, immeasurable,
the sorrows of the world came settling then
draped like an old coat that cannot be mended

but can't be let go—sodden wool.
The weight of too much sorry news piled
story on story, dulling my mind,

an inner echo of the world's gray. Then
the sun pushed light fingers through the tired air
touched the long hair of the beaten old fen,

warmed the bark on the tree where I leaned.
I lay myself down on the matted ground
felt as my weight was caught and cradled.

The heavy shadows slid off beneath me
to dissolve into loam that does, after all,
swallow all our sorrows in the end, and kindly.

A scarlet dragonfly flickered and rose
to the living wood by the side of my face.
She danced up and down on the tips of her toes

shaking her glimmering wings, she tilted
the small dark marble of her head back and forth,
the red line of her body a shiver of light.

Lightly she raised her shining wings
to carry her down to my folded hands.
One heartbeat, two, she passed the blessing

then floated away, ruby gleam of a gift.
In the light left behind I could see my true life:
one quiet thing at a time.

THIS PLACE IS SANCTUARY

You who are broken-hearted,
who woke today with the winds of despair
whistling through your mind,
come in.
You who are brave but wounded,
limping through life and hurting with every step,
come in.
You who are fearful, who live with shadows
hovering over your shoulders,
come in.
This place is sanctuary, and it is for you.
You who are filled with happiness,
whose abundance overflows,
come in.
You who walk through your world
with lightness and grace,
who awoke this morning with strength and hope,
you who have everything to give,
come in.
This place is your calling, a riverbank to channel
the sweet waters of your life, the place
where you are called by the world's need.
Here we offer in love.
Here we receive in gratitude.
Here we make a circle from the great gifts
of breath, attention and purpose.
Come in.

WHO KNOWS YOU?

Some of the old New England graveyards are serene
little pockets of neglect. Their slate tombstones lean
at odd angles and the elegant calligraphy is barely
legible, spelling out obscure colonial names like
"Ozias" and "Zebulon." Some of the inscriptions that
can still be deciphered tell poignant stories of sons
and husbands fallen in long-ago wars and young
wives lost in childbirth. Clusters of brick-sized stones
mark the deaths of children in some catastrophic
winter. The engraved cries of lament—"Farewell,
Beloved Daughter"—evoke a tug of grief even now,
though the people named have been dust and earth
for two hundred years or more.

One of these graveyards in my town evokes a
sadness of a different sort, held in the inscription on
a modern tombstone marking the resting place of
Franklin F. Bailey. He was born in 1901 and buried in
1988, so he lived a long time. His epitaph says simply,
"Here lies a man that nobody really knew."

What a strange message to leave echoing down
through the years—and what a freight of sadness is
held in that short phrase! It tells of isolation, loneliness, a life lived invisibly, a voice unheard. "Here lies
a man that nobody really knew."

Who knows you? We each move through the
world caught within the bubble of our own mind,

circling around each other like small planets on which each of us is the only citizen. Spiritual practices are meant to turn us directly into that inner landscape, so we can know it well and without illusion. But their larger purpose is to show us pathways to one another, because with practice we come to know a bedrock truth of this human life: However different each inner landscape is from the others, the same winds blow through us all. They are the winds of longing and fear, doubt, hope and regret. No one is exempt. That simple recognition opens a deep well of compassion, both for our own struggles and for those taking place behind all the faces that surround us.

I wonder about Franklin Bailey every time I take a walk through that little graveyard. I also wonder about the Franklin Baileys who walk among us. Who today is living a life of unremitting loneliness, in my town, in my neighborhood, perhaps even in my own family? Before it comes time for a sad epitaph summing up their isolation, perhaps we can extend a bridge of compassion, allowing them to feel seen, heard, and touched—to be known a little, in the brief, common walk of our lives.

MASKS AND REVELATIONS

It was a few days after Halloween and I had just
retrieved my daughters from their daycare. As
we drove home in the early darkness we passed a
house with a big picture window, lit up from within.
My daughter Hannah was not yet three years old,
and she practiced her vocabulary through a run-
ning commentary on the world as it went past. She
announced from the back seat, "Mommy, that house
had two peoples and a dog in it." Thinking about
Halloween and all the decorations that were still
around, I asked absently, "Were they real or pretend?" She answered firmly, "They were real."

Ten minutes later when we were nearly to our
own driveway and my mind had drifted far afield,
her voice again floated out from the back seat.
"Mommy, are we real or pretend?" I suddenly felt
the ear of God inclined toward me. Is this a simple
question of information, or is it a theological test?
A three-year-old isn't looking for an existential
discourse, but long after the child has left the question and its simple answer behind her, an echo still
dances around in the psyche.

Are you real, or pretend? Probably a little of
both. It's a rare and saintly person who can bring
forth a depth of authenticity to every moment. Quite
aside from the easy masks we might play with on

Halloween, we run the risk of getting caught up in more serious disguises, all those images we can carry around in our minds without even being aware of it. Maybe it's our idea of the perfect mother or the dutiful son, the beloved teacher or pious minister, the skilled social worker or respected CEO—whatever it is we hope the world will see when it looks at us. When we confuse what we do with who we are, are we real? Or are we pretend?

How about the rest of the lives around us. Are they real to us? The people caught in traffic in the car next to you, the waiter who just took your order, the woman who cleans your work space after you've gone home for the day—are they completely real to you? Consider those far away in terms of geography, belief, or circumstance. The people suffering in Haiti, Palestine, or Pakistan, the hundreds of thousands of men imprisoned in our own country, the homeless woman on a bench downtown, or those who come to mind when we hear words like *Muslim* or *evangelical* or *conservative*. Are they real, or are they pretend? Do we let them blossom into genuine human beings who are complex, maddening, unpredictable, and different from us—or do we reduce them to parodies, people we can dismiss, who we can easily call our enemy?

Sometimes we put on our own masks. Sometimes we put masks on other people. One of the purposes of a spiritual life is to help us engage deeply in the search for truth. Sometimes that search is sharpened and focused by the query of a child, ringing out like the sound of a meditation bell.

Are you real, or pretend?

THE MEDICINE IS IN THE ALTAR

The ancient Irish believed that around this time of year, as autumn tips toward winter, the veils that separate the living from the dead begin to thin and vanish, and that if we listen carefully enough we might even hear again from those we've lost.

Don't we all sometimes have an intuition of this mysterious idea? I know a man who lost his teenaged son in a car accident. In the terrible days immediately following, he woke at dawn every morning with a powerful sense that his son was sitting calmly on the edge of the bed, tenderly resting his hand on his father's shoulder. My friend doesn't believe in this sort of thing. He doesn't believe the dead visit us, in any form. Yet he says the physical sense of that warm weight resting on his shoulder was so vivid that he woke those mornings not only with his searing grief, but with a strange sense of peace and indelible connection.

Our world is filled with stories like this one: How do we understand them? Are they ghost stories, imagination, tricks of the mind, delusion? Or is it truer, though perhaps less comfortable, to simply admit that there is a whole universe of knowledge that is not ours, at least not yet, and that the kingdom of death is in that universe? What do we really know about death, except that we'll each take our turn walking through its shadowed gate?

I sat by my father's bed as he moved through the last days and nights of his life. It was intense and painful. It was also wondrous and awesome to hold his hand as the light left his eyes. In the weeks that followed I struggled with my grief, and then my father showed up in a dream so powerful it felt like a visitation. In the dream he was thin and sick, standing by a bureau with his back to me. As I entered the room my greeting startled him, so that a huge collection of pills he had been arranging scattered from his hands and fell.

"Pick them up!" he demanded. As I bent to do it, I saw that the pills had all fallen onto the little altar which in waking life sits in my home as the focus of my meditation practice. There the pills had mingled with the small shiny stones I've collected from far away beaches, and as I looked I saw it would be impossible to separate them out from each other. That's all there was. I awoke from the dream and immediately said to myself, "The medicine is in the altar." Though I often disagreed with my father while he lived and just as often ignored his advice, this dream father gave me a reminder I needed to hear. In the quiet of meditation, I found the comfort that sustained me through the worst of my grieving.

"What do you think has become of the young and old men? And what do you think has become of the women and children?" asks Walt Whitman in *Leaves of Grass*. Surely we carry them with us. Their wisdom and love are rooted in our own minds and hearts, rising to the surface unexpectedly from time to time, mingled inseparably with our own thoughts and visions. The great cloud of witnesses who have lived and died before us breathe out to us in all the forms of life our sweet world devises. They are all around us. The ancient Celts had it right. The separation between the living and the dead is thin as a veil, but not just in the darkening of the year. It's always there. If we quiet ourselves enough we can still hear their voices, there in our own heart's beating.

VETERANS' DAY PRAYER IN A TIME OF WAR

Light a candle to name this hollow sadness,
to name the fear, and the tendrils of despair.
Watch the fragile light flickering there, and promise
    in the name of all that is holy
that you will shelter within yourself an answering
    flame:
    the call of peace, the insistence on peace,
setting other lights ablaze for as long as it will take.

Pray for the soldiers of our country,
warriors who battle in our name.
They are so young, these sons, these daughters.
They are afraid they will be killed,
afraid they will do grievous harm.
They are frightened of failure,
    and of what they must do
    to succeed.
Pray for the safety of their bodies and the wholeness
    of their spirits;
pray for some comfort to touch the ones
    who love them.

Pray for the soldiers of our enemy,
whose names are shaped by a foreign tongue.
Pray for their safety and wholeness as well.

Pray to remember that these are our brothers:
    they bleed when they are wounded,
    their hearts break in sorrow.
Like us, they long for a gentler day
when they might wake to the morning in peace
and know themselves to be safe.

Light a candle in a time of war.
Do not hide from the truth of what unfolds now
on the far side of the sweetly spinning earth.
Remember: swords do not shape themselves
    into plowshares.
That work is in our hands.

TENDING THE SECRET GARDEN

It was a soggy November morning. The leaves had all fallen from the trees and the woods were darkened by days of rain. A high overcast dimmed the sun, so everything in sight reflected the dulled colors of early winter: brown and gray, drab greens and faded yellows. It was a disheartening scene, with the promise of weeks more to come until the winter snow would soften the lines and lift the light. Then as I stared through the window at this bleak view, feeling more than a little dull and gray myself, a pair of bluebirds flew to a branch directly at eye level, flashing almost neon in their brightness.

The "bluebird of happiness" has never been an image that worked very well for me—much too saccharine, like those awful yellow smiley-face buttons. Yet I have to admit, my heart did a little flip-flop of joy when those beautiful creatures lit up the landscape. They danced their jaunty bird jig on the branch for a few minutes and then flew away, but the landscape held a sheen I hadn't noticed before, a little backwash of light left behind.

On the wall above my desk I keep a favorite quote by Sarah Brethnach: "Both abundance and lack exist simultaneously in our lives, as parallel realities. It is always our conscious choice which secret garden we will tend."

So often we take meticulous care of the Garden of Dissatisfaction, cultivated from every lack in our lives. We leave its gate wide open and we wander in each morning almost before we're fully awake, already sorry for ourselves because we didn't sleep well again, or the weather is foul, or work feels like too much of a grind. We linger in the Garden of Dissatisfaction, usually without even noticing we've made a choice. We return again and again to the unkempt and extravagant growth of our favorite gripes, some of them many years old and still full of whining vigor.

But there's another garden growing right alongside this one, and just a small shift of perspective tumbles us into its grace. In the Garden of Abundance, the landscape overflows with the ordinary miracles that shimmer through each day we are privileged to walk in this world. This garden grows easily, it blossoms freely, and its richness awaits us each time we open our eyes to see it: life, breath, kindness, friends, love. Bluebirds. All the bounty given to us by every unfolding day.

In the Garden of Abundance, the bare branches against a November overcast become a blessing, not because of the bluebirds that lighted there for a moment but because the branches themselves exist, and we have the eyes to see them, outlined against the soft, beautiful gray of the sky. Which secret garden will you tend today?

THANKSGIVING BENEDICTION

What question do you think you need answered
in order to wake to the morning
and step into your life with joy?

Listen:
the dark branches scrolled sharp against a pure sky
are the only map you will ever receive.

When you look at those lines, when you
    attend to them
until you feel yourself lifted by their dark runes
into the clear winter sun
or the dimming light of evening,
there is your guide.

When gratitude rises as the only prayer of your heart,
you are learning, at last,
what it is to be fully alive.

SAYING GRACE

Wise women and men from every tradition teach
that gratitude is at the heart of the spiritual life
because it leads us to all the rest. Consider the sim-
plest practice of gratitude, saying grace before we eat
a meal. That little moment of attention is enough to
wake us up to the world. Instead of chugging a glass
of water down our thirsty throats, gratitude reminds
us how lucky we are that clean water flows for us
with the simple turn of the handle at a sink. Instead
of packing in our food so we can get on to the next
activity or eating so distractedly that we barely taste
it, that moment of saying grace helps us look at the
meal with a kind of reverence. We pause and remember not everyone gets to eat. Not even everyone in
our country, in our own city, gets to eat.

Where did it all come from, this food, this water?
None of it spontaneously generated there on the
plate or in the glass. So we remember the rain and
soil and sun on which everything depends. We
remember the invisible makers of this meal, the people who bend over the fields for hours planting or
harvesting, the ones in the barns or slaughterhouses,
the ones who work in factories or who drive the
trucks or ring up the cash registers. Even a fleeting
prayer of thankfulness for our daily bread reminds
us of how fragile and dependent our bodies are, how

everything hinges on everything else, and awakens us again to the fundamental grace of breath, water, food.

Thank you for the earth, the sun, and rain.
Thank you for the gladness of being together
    at this table.
May they be blessed, all those whose hands
planted, nurtured, harvested, and helped
    to prepare this food.
May it make us strong for the work of our world. Amen.

ON THE CUSP OF WINTER

We've come to the season of waiting.
The colors of autumn are gone,
leaves faded and fallen, and branches rise bare
to the sky.
The deep quiet and frozen beauty of winter are
     coming
but not quite yet: we are in the season in between.

The world closes in on itself as breathing things
hunker down, burrow in, drop to the bottom
and store up nurture for the long cold.

Animals that we are, we feel in our bones
the shuttering of the windows.
Though freed from the need to burrow in,
may we still find guidance
in the rhythm that beats through our hearts.

In this season of waiting, may we let ourselves
slow down our pace,
ease out from beneath the burden of our speed
and bustle, our fretful worry
so that gratitude can saturate our days and color our
     nights.

In this season of closing down, closing in,
may our hearts stay open,

urging open our doors to the stranger, our hands
to the helpless,
and our spirits to all that calls us endlessly back to life.

THE PARENTS' PILGRIMAGE

On the day my first child greeted the light of the
world and was lifted into my arms, I had no clue
about the impact she would have on my spiritual life.
I would have told anyone who asked that this child
was God Herself, or as near to it as I would ever get,
and she immediately became the focus for my pas-
sionate idolatry.

I lived in a state of awe during the early weeks of
her life. In the long silences of night-time nursing
and through days that drifted and eddied around
this new being, no detail could escape my attention.
I was mesmerized by her minute fingernails, the
curve of her foot, the perfect translucence of her
ear, the blue-black depth of her eyes. Through all
my years working with various spiritual disciplines
of prayer and meditation, the heart of the practice
was always to learn deeper attention. After my baby's
birth, attention flowed effortlessly, expanding out
from the center she occupied like ripples on a pond.

I suppose if those early days fully characterized
parenting, people raising children would all be on
the fast track to enlightenment, but the path doesn't
stay within that surreal realm for very long, and the
new parent soon understands why there are so few
stories of saints outside of the monastic tradition.
Along with the profound joy of parenting come all
those other experiences that interrupt our starry-

eyed devotion: the drool and spit-up, the months of sleep deprivation, the endless diapers and, for some unlucky souls, the mind-numbing nights of colic. Later on there are squabbles and tantrums, the willful deafness to parental pleas, the high-pitched scream in inhuman decibels. Above all there is the constancy of interruption: broken sleep and fragmented dreams, conversations reduced to half-sentence snippets, days divided into fractions, each part full of uncompleted tasks.

The spiritual life is usually depicted as requiring total dedication: the solitary pilgrimage, the focused weeks of prayer or meditation, the ecstatic chanting in the company of other seekers. When Siddhartha began the journey that would transform him into the Buddha, he left behind his wife and infant son. This choice seems unforgivable, hardly the stuff of enlightenment, but on the classic spiritual journey, characterized by austerity and solitude, there is no room for spouse and baby to trot alongside.

We don't hear stories about saints and sages walking the path to their enlightenment hauling bags of diapers and stacks of diaper wipes, liquid Tylenol and teething rings. It's hard to imagine them engaging in soul-deepening religious thought or dialogue while wiping a runny nose or cleaning up after Spaghetti-Os. Parents are more likely to be poring time and again over the words of *The Runaway Bunny* or *Goodnight Moon* than the classic sacred texts.

The real journey with children is motivated not by our spiritual hungers but by our offspring's more prosaic appetites. Parents have little opportunity for regular prayer or meditation, Sabbath reflection, study or journal-writing. Instead, their journey leads right through the life we are living—through the chaos, the interruptions, the exhaustion.

This ordinary, unsung path requires tremendous openness to the unanticipated. It meanders around a thousand turns that feel like detours or dead ends. It requires faith that the spirit does not grow in a straight line nor need traditional forms and practices. Real spiritual growth depends on our willingness to be transformed, and very little transforms us as thoroughly as sharing our lives with children.

HANUKKAH

Imagine yourself in the midst of the ancient story. You and your friends, the survivors of war and persecution, have finally come home from a hard-won victory, but it doesn't feel like home. It has been shifted, cracked and broken by war, and it's shadowed by the ghosts of those who have died. You all teeter on the edge of despair when you see the temple, the holy of holies, filthy and abused. Your arms ache at even the thought of what it takes to reclaim this space. In any case, what's the use? The sacred oil is almost gone, so the consecrating lamp cannot be lit.

Then, in the midst of the exhausted, grieving silence, someone speaks. You hear the voice, small but firm, saying the only words that will let you gather yourselves to go on: *Light the lamp. Though the oil has run out, light the lamp anyway, and we'll do what we can.*

On the wall next to my meditation altar there is a photo taken in the wake of the horrifying tsunami that struck Sri Lanka in 2004. The photo shows the ruins of a town flattened by the waters, nothing left but rubble, and there in the midst of that devastation, a damaged statue of the Buddha has been set upright, its carved face chipped but still beautiful and serene. It sits there like a beacon sending out the silent message: *Life is still here. Begin again.*

In Haiti on the night after the catastrophic earthquake that took so many lives and leveled a city, in the utter darkness of a place in which there was no electricity, thousands of survivors in Port au Prince gathered at the shells of their churches. They stood in the night all around their shattered spiritual homes, lifted their voices, and sang. They poured out sacred songs of praise, of lamentation, and of hope.

What were they doing, the people of Sri Lanka who set the statue amidst the rubble, the people of Haiti who lifted their voices against the earthquake? They were lighting the lamps, even though they knew that their oil had run out.

There will come a time for most of us when we've got to decide whether we'll light our lamps, even when we're sure there isn't enough oil to keep them burning. It doesn't take a literal earthquake or flood for our lives to be swept away. There are other, smaller catastrophes: the long weariness of unemployment; sickness, bereavement, depression; or the other private disasters that make us despair.

In the face of these smaller floods and earthquakes, we come back to sacred space. We light a candle, take a breath, and reconnect with the flow of a life infinitely larger than our little beating hearts—a life we are part of no matter what, that calls us back, lifts us up, and sustains us.

Light the lamp, though the oil has run out. Light the lamp, and we'll do what we can.

CHRISTMAS EVE

All these centuries after the story of the star,
the wise men, the baby born in the stable
and the angels singing him in with their
    mysterious alleluias,
we are lost and wandering still.
We stumble at every step
over our own greed or need, our ignorance or fear.

Bethlehem is not a gentle city tonight.
Its people are wise in the ways of the clenched fist,
    the broken truce.
Marked like them with the scars of ignorance and
    sorrow
we come to Christmas baffled as any shepherd
by the music that sounds so high above us,
the syntax foreign to our skeptical hearts.

Yet we try to speak the language of hope,
lifting ourselves toward the future with a dream
of what yet may be.

We remember that the heart of Christmas is hope:
hope that a child, born homeless and in danger,
may grow up to be wise and kind;
that the stars, serene in their darkness,
have something to teach;
that there are mysteries around us, among us, singing
    ethereal harmonies.

New hope in ourselves rises then, too:
that we will learn, one day,
and in the nick of time, how to walk our paths
with truth and justice, how to bring peace
to life on this earth,
how to sing for ourselves the angels' songs
of praise, wonder and joy.

Unitarians and Universalists have been publishing prayer collections and meditation manuals for more than 170 years. In 1841 the Unitarians broke with their tradition of addressing only theological topics and published *Short Prayers for the Morning and Evening of Every Day in the Week, with Occasional Prayers and Thanksgivings.* Over the years, the Unitarians published many more volumes of prayers, including Theodore Parker's selections. In 1938 *Gaining a Radiant Faith* by Henry H. Saunderson launched the tradition of an annual Lenten manual.

Several Universalist collections appeared in the early nineteenth century. A comprehensive Book of Prayers was published in 1839, featuring both public and private devotions. Like the Unitarians, the Universalists published Lenten manuals, and in the 1950s they complemented this series with Advent manuals.

Since 1961, the year the Unitarians and Universalists consolidated, the Lenten manual has evolved into a meditation manual.

For a complete list of meditation manuals, please visit
www.uua.org/skinner/meditation